M000276357

XAMonline, Inc.
25 First Street, Suite 106
Cambridge, MA 02141
Toll Free: 1-800-509-4128
Email: info@xamonline.com
Web: www.xamonline.com
Fax: 1-617-583-5552

Library of Congress Cataloging-in-Publication Data

Wynne, Sharon A.
    WEST-E Special Education Practice Test 1: Teacher Certification /
    Sharon A. Wynne. -1st ed.
    ISBN: 978-1-60787-303-7
    1. WEST-E Special Education Practice Test 1
    2. Study Guides   3. WEST-E   4. Teachers' Certification & Licensure
    5. Careers

Disclaimer:
The opinions expressed in this publication are the sole works of XAMonline and were created
independently from the National Education Association, Educational Testing Service, or any
State Department of Education, National Evaluation Systems or other testing affiliates.

Between the time of publication and printing, state specific standards as well as testing
formats and website information may change that is not included in part or in whole within this
product. Sample test questions are developed by XAMonline and reflect similar content as on
real tests; however, they are not former tests. XAMonline assembles content that aligns with
state standards but makes no claims nor guarantees teacher candidates a passing score.
Numerical scores are determined by testing companies such as NES or ETS and then are
compared with individual state standards. A passing score varies from state to state.

Printed in the United States of America   œ-1
WEST-E Special Education Practice Test 1
ISBN: 978-1-60787-303-7

UNDERSTANDING EXCEPTIONALITIES

1. **All of the following EXCEPT one are characteristics of a student who is Emotionally Disturbed:**
   (Average)

   A. Socially accepted by peers

   B. Highly disruptive to the classroom environment

   C. Academic difficulties

   D. Areas of talent overlooked by a teacher

2. **Which of these characteristics is NOT included in the IDEA definition of emotional disturbance?**
   (Rigorous)

   A. General pervasive mood of unhappiness or depression

   B. Social maladjustment manifested in a number of settings

   C. Tendency to develop physical symptoms, pains, or fear associated with school or personal problems

   D. Inability to learn that is not attributed to intellectual, sensory, or health factors

3. **Truancy, gang membership, and a feeling of pride in belonging to a delinquent subculture are indicative of:**
   (Average)

   A. Conduct disorder

   B. Personality disorders

   C. Immaturity

   D. Socialized aggression

4. **Indirect requests and attempts to influence or control others through one's use of language is an example of:**
   (Rigorous)

   A. Morphology

   B. Syntax

   C. Pragmatics

   D. Semantics

5. Scott is in middle school but still makes statements like, "I gotted new high-tops yesterday," and "I saw three mans in the front office." Language interventions for Scott would target:
(Average)

   A. Morphology

   B. Syntax

   C. Pragmatics

   D. Semantics

6. Which component of language involves language content rather than the form of language?
(Rigorous)

   A. Phonology

   B. Morphology

   C. Semantics

   D. Syntax

7. Which of the following characteristics is probably most related to physical impairments?
(Rigorous)

   A. Lack of physical stamina

   B. Progressive weakening of muscles

   C. Impaired motor abilities

   D. Side effects from treatment

8. Jennifer is eight years old and has been diagnosed with Mental Retardation. She exhibits the following characteristics: poor motor development, minimal speech and communication, is not potty trained, and requires constant supervision. How would she be classified in terms of degree of cognitive impairment?
(Rigorous)

   A. Mild

   B. Moderate

   C. Severe

   D. Profound

9. Otumba is a 16 year old in your class who recently came from Nigeria. The girls in your class have come to you to complain about the way he treats them in a sexist manner. When they complain you reflect that this is also the way he treats adult females. You have talked to Otumba before about appropriate behavior. You should first:
(Rigorous)

   A. Complain to the Principal

   B. Ask for a Parent-Teacher Conference

   C. Check to see if this is a cultural norm in his country

   D. Create a behavior contract for him to follow

10. Some of the factors that can contribute to learning disabilities and/or cognitive impairments include problems with fetal brain development, genetic factors, environmental factors, problems during pregnancy or delivery, environmental toxins, and the use of drugs or alcohol during pregnancy. Which of the following conditions can be directly related to one of the above listed factors? (*Easy*)

A. Emotional Disturbance

B. Fetal Alcohol Syndrome

C. Learning Disability

D. Attention Deficit Disorder

11. Statements like, "Darren is lazy," are not helpful in describing his behavior for all but which of these reasons? (*Rigorous*)

A. There is no way to determine if any change occurs from the information given

B. The student and not the behavior becomes labeled

C. Darren's behavior will manifest itself clearly enough without any written description

D. Such labels are open to various interpretations among the people who are asked to define them

12. Criteria for choosing behaviors that most need change involve all but the following: (*Average*)

A. Observations across settings to rule out certain interventions

B. Pinpointing the behavior that is the poorest fit in the child's environment

C. The teacher's concern about what is the most important behavior to target

D. Analysis of the environmental reinforcers

13. Measuring frequency is appropriate for all of these behaviors EXCEPT: (*Rigorous*)

A. Teasing

B. Talking out

C. Being on time for class

D. Off-task behavior

14. **Which is generally true about students with mild disabilities?**
    (Easy)

    A. Comprise about half of the total special education population

    B. Are generally recognized once they begin school and have learning challenges

    C. Have a high school dropout rate

    D. All of the above

15. **Which of the following is true about autism?**
    (Rigorous)

    A. It is caused by having cold, aloof or hostile parents

    B. Approximately 4 out of 10 people have autism

    C. It is a Separate Exceptionality Category in IDEA

    D. It is a form of Mental Illness

16. **In which of the following exceptionality categories may a student be considered for inclusion if his IQ score falls more than two standard deviations below the mean?**
    (Average)

    A. Mental Retardation

    B. Specific Learning Disabilities

    C. Emotionally/Behaviorally Disordered

    D. Gifted

17. **According to IDEA, a child whose disability is related to being deaf and blind may not be classified as:**
    (Rigorous)

    A. Multiple Disabilities

    B. Other Health Impaired

    C. Mentally Retarded

    D. Visually Impaired

18. **Legislation in Public Law 94 – 142 attempts to:**
    (Average Rigor)

    A. Match the child's educational needs with appropriate educational services

    B. Include parents in the decisions made about their child's education

    C. Establish a means by which parents can provide input

    D. All of the above

19. **The definition of assistive technology devices was amended in the IDEA reauthorization of 2004 to exclude what?**
    (Average)

    A. iPods and other hand-held devices

    B. Computer enhanced technology

    C. Surgically implanted devices

    D. Braille and/or special learning aids

20. **The Individuals with Disabilities Education Act (IDEA) was signed into law in:**
    (Average)

    A. 1975

    B. 1980

    C. 1990

    D. 1995

21. **Section 504 differs from the scope of IDEA because its main focus is on:**
    (Rigorous)

    A. Prohibition of discrimination on the basis of disability

    B. A basis for additional support services and accommodations in a special education setting

    C. Procedural rights and safeguards for the individual

    D. Federal funding for educational services

22. **Satisfaction of the Least Restrictive Environment (LRE) requirement means:**
(Rigorous)

A. The school is providing the best services it can offer

B. The school is providing the best services the district has to offer

C. The student is being educated with the fewest special education services necessary

D. The student is being educated in the least restrictive setting that meets his or her needs

23. **What legislation started FAPE?**
(Rigorous)

A. Section 504

B. EHCA

C. IDEA

D. Education Amendment 1974

24. **Which is untrue about the Americans with disabilities Act (ADA)?**
(Rigorous)

A. It was signed into law the same year as IDEA by President Bush

B. It reauthorized the discretionary programs of EHA

C It gives protection to all people on the basis of race, sex, national origin, and religion

D. It guarantees equal opportunities to persons with disabilities in employment, public accommodations, transportation, government services, and telecommunications

25. **One of the most important goals of the special education teacher is to foster and create with the student:**
(Easy)

A. Handwriting skills

B. Self-advocacy

C. An increased level of reading

D. Logical reasoning

26. **The best resource a teacher can have to reach a student is:**
(Rigorous)

   A. Contact with the parents/guardians

   B. A successful behavior modification exam

   C. A listening ear

   D. Gathered scaffold approach to teaching

27. **The earliest establishment of organizations whose membership contained professionals in related fields serving individuals with disabilities came from:**
(Rigorous)

   A. Sociology

   B. Psychology

   C. Medicine

   D. All of the Above

28. **The service medium facility that helps formerly institutionalized clients to adjust while becoming self-supporting members of the community is the:**
(Rigorous)

   A. Half-way Residential Home

   B. Group Home

   C. Sheltered Workshop

   D. Foster Family Home

29. **Which is a less than ideal example of collaboration for successful inclusion?**
(Average)

   A. Special education teachers are part of the instructional team in a regular classroom

   B. Special education teachers act as assistants to regular education teachers in the classroom

   C. Teaming approaches are used for problem solving and program implementation

   D. Regular teachers, special education teachers, and other specialists or support teachers co-teach

30. **The movement towards serving as many children with disabilities as possible in the regular classroom with supports and services grew out of:**
(Average)

   A. The Full Service Model

   B. The Regular Education Model

   C. The Normalization movement

   D. The Mainstream Model

DELIVERY OF SERVICES TO STUDENTS

31. **Cognitive Learning strategies include:**
(Rigorous)

   A. Reinforcing appropriate behavior

   B. Teaching students problem solving and critical thinking skills

   C. Heavily structuring the learning environment

   D. Generalizing learning from one setting to another

32. **Bob shows behavior problems such as lack of attention, out of seat, and talking out. His teacher has kept data on these behaviors and has found that Bob is showing much better self-control since he has been self-managing himself through a behavior modification program. The most appropriate placement recommendation for Bob at this time is probably:**
(Easy)

   A. Any available part-time special education program

   B. The regular classroom solely

   C. A behavior disorders resource room for one period a day

   D. A specific learning disabilities resource room for one period a day

33. **A important component of IDEA deals with "Due Process." Due Process a set of procedures designed to ensure fairness and accountability in decisions related to the education of students with disabilities. Which of the following is NOT considered a Due Process right for parents under IDEA?**
(Average)

   A. The right to specify which school personnel will work with their child

   B. The right to a Due Process Hearing if they do not agree with the school's recommendations

   C. The right to an Independent Educational Evaluation (IEE)

   D. The right to written notice prior to a prior to a proposal or refusal to initiate or make a change in the child's identification, evaluation, or educational placement

34. **The effective teacher varies her instructional presentations and response requirements depending upon:**
(Easy)

   A. Student needs

   B. The task at hand

   C. The learning situation

   D. All of the above

35. The following words describe an IEP objective EXCEPT:
(Average)

A. Specific

B. Observable

C. Measurable

D. Criterion-referenced

36. Which one of the following is NOT a primary purpose of an IEP?
(Rigorous)

A. To outline instructional programs

B. To develop self-advocacy skills

C. To function as the basis for evaluation

D. To facilitate communication among staff members, teachers, parents, and students

37. _____ is a method used to increase student engaged learning time by having students teach other students.
(Easy)

A. Peer tutoring

B. Engaged learning time

C. Allocated learning time

D. Teacher consultation

38. The Integrated approach to learning utilizes all resources available to address student needs. What are the resources?
(Rigorous)

A. The student, his/her parents, and the teacher

B. The teacher, the parents, and the special education team

C. The teacher, the student, and an administrator to perform needed interventions

D. The student, his/her parents, the teacher, and community resources

39. Cooperative learning uses all these methods, EXCEPT:
(Average)

A. Shared ideas

B. Small groups

C. Independent practice

D. Student expertise

40. **Presentation of tasks can be altered to match the student's rate of learning by:**
(Rigorous)

A. Describing how much of a topic is presented in one day, and how much practice is assigned, according to the student's abilities and learning style

B. Using task analysis, assign a certain number of skills to be mastered in a specific amount of time

C. Introducing a new task only when the student has demonstrated mastery of the previous task in the learning hierarchy

D. A and C

41. **Alternative response patterns are educationally important because:**
(Easy)

A. They allow the special needs student the opportunity to approach a task from a position that best suits his learning style

B. They permit the teacher to use her knowledge of the students' learning styles and capabilities to design the best learning environment for each student

C. They allow all students, even non-readers, to interact in the instructional setting

D. All of the above

42. **Which type of instructional arrangement established and enhances mutual respect for other students and promotes positive social goals:**
(Rigorous)

A. Homogeneous grouping

B. One-on-one instruction

C. Cooperative learning

D. Small group instruction

43. **Functional skills include _____ skills.**
(Easy)

A. personal-social

B. daily living

C. occupational readiness

D. All of the above

44. **In career education, specific training and preparation required for the world of work occurs during the phase of:**
(Easy)

A. Career Awareness

B. Career Exploration

C. Career Preparation

D. Daily Living and Personal-Social Interaction

45. For which stage of learning would computer software be utilized that allows for continued drill and practice of a skill to achieve accuracy and speed?
(Average)

A. Acquisition

B. Proficiency

C. Maintenance

D. Generalization

46. When a student begins to use assistive technology, it is important for the teacher to have a clear outline as to when and how the equipment should be used. Why?
(Rigorous)

A. To establish a level of accountability with the student

B. To establish that the teacher has responsibility for the equipment that is in use in his/her room

C. To establish that the teacher is responsible for the usage of the assistive technology

D. To establish a guideline for evaluation

47. Which is characteristic of standardized group tests?
(Rigorous)

A. Directions are always read to students

B. The examiner monitors several students at the same time

C. The teacher is allowed to probe students who almost have the correct answer

D. Both quantitative and qualitative information may be gathered

48. Which of the following types of tests is used to estimate learning potential and to predict academic achievement?
(Easy)

A. Intelligence Tests

B. Achievement Tests

C. Adaptive Behavior Tests

D. Personality Tests

49. In exceptional student education, assessment is used to make decisions about all of the following except:
(Average)

A. Screening and initial identification of children who may need services

B. Selection and evaluation of teaching strategies and programs

C. Determining the desired attendance rate of a student

D. Development of goals, objectives, and evaluation for the IEP

50. Children who write poorly might be given tests that allow oral responses, unless the purpose for giving the test is to:
(Easy)

A. Assess handwriting skills

B. Test for organization of thoughts

C. Answer questions pertaining to math reasoning

D. Assess rote memory

51. Alternative assessments include all of the following EXCEPT:
(Average)

A. Portfolios

B. Interviews

C. Textbook chapter tests

D. Student choice of assessment format

52. According to Mercer and Mercer, what would be an appropriate amount of homework for a student in fourth grade:
(Average)

A. 15 minutes, 3 days a week

B. 45–75 minutes, 5 days a week

C. 75–120 minutes, 5 days a week

D. 15–45 minutes, 2 to 4 days a week

53. Mr. Brown finds that his chosen consequence does not seem to be having the desired effect of reducing the target misbehavior. Which of these would LEAST LIKELY account for Mr. Brown's lack of success with the consequence?
(Easy)

A. The consequence was aversive in Mr. Brown's opinion but not the students'

B. The students were not developmentally ready to understand the connection

C. Mr. Brown was inconsistent in applying the consequence

D. The intervention had not previously been shown to be effective in studies

54. When would proximity control not be a good behavioral intervention?
(Easy)

A. Two students are arguing

B. A student is distracting others

C. One student threatens another

D. Involve fading and shaping

55. Katie frequently is disruptive prior to each day's math lesson. From a behavior management perspective, the math lesson appears to be the _____ to Katie's undesirable disruptive behavior.
(Average)

A. subsequent development

B. succeeding force

C. consequence

D. antecedent

56. The best way to ensure the success of educational interventions is to:
(Average)

A. Give regular education teachers the primary responsibility of teaching special needs students in regular classrooms

B. Give special education teachers the primary responsibility of teaching special needs students in special education classrooms

C. Promote cooperative teaching efforts between general and special educators

D. Have support personnel assume the primary responsibility for the Education of special needs students

57. In regard to the influence of teacher attitudes, which of the following is critical in the successful inclusion of the student with a disability: *(Average)*

A. The special education teacher should take full responsibility for the student with a disability

B. The student with a disability only attend special events with the general education classroom

C. Special education and regular education teachers should demonstrate the attitude that the exceptional student is a student of both teachers, not a special education student who only goes into a general education classroom at certain times

D. The general education should wait for the special education teacher to be in the classroom before interacting with the student

58. Which of the following would promote a good working relationship with a paraprofessional who has been assigned to your classroom? *(Average)*

A. Having the paraprofessional grade papers

B. Telling the paraprofessional what you expect him/her to do

C. Offering support to paraprofessionals by observing their work with students and offering feedback and suggestions

D. Asking the paraprofessional to sit in the back of the room and only interact with students when you direct them

59. Related service providers include all of the following EXCEPT: *(Average)*

A. General education teachers

B. Speech and language therapists

C. Occupational therapists

D. Psychologists

60. In conducting a parent conference, the teacher should address each of the following EXCEPT:
(Easy)

A. Provide samples of student work and other relevant information

B. Focus on observable behaviors

C. Offer suggestions for better parenting

D. Be a good listener

Special Education
Pre-Test Sample Questions with Rationales

UNDERSTANDING EXCEPTIONALITIES

1. **All of the following EXCEPT one are characteristics of a student who is Emotionally Disturbed:**
   (Average)

   A. Socially accepted by peers

   B. Highly disruptive to the classroom environment

   C. Academic difficulties

   D. Areas of talent overlooked by a teacher

   Answer: A. Socially accepted by peers
   While a such a child **may** be socially accepted by peers, children who are emotionally disturbed tend to alienate those around them and are often ostracized.

2. **Which of these characteristics is NOT included in the IDEA definition of emotional disturbance?**
   (Rigorous)

   A. General pervasive mood of unhappiness or depression

   B. Social maladjustment manifested in a number of settings

   C. Tendency to develop physical symptoms, pains, or fear associated with school or personal problems

   D. Inability to learn that is not attributed to intellectual, sensory, or health factors

   Answer: B. Social maladjustment manifested in a number of settings
   Social maladjustment is not considered a disability.

3. **Truancy, gang membership, and a feeling of pride in belonging to a delinquent subculture are indicative of:**
(Average)

  A.   Conduct disorder

  B.   Personality disorders

  C.   Immaturity

  D.   Socialized aggression

Answer: D. Socialized aggression
The student is acting out by using aggression. This gives him a sense of belonging.

4. **Indirect requests and attempts to influence or control others through one's use of language is an example of:**
(Rigorous)

  A.   Morphology

  B.   Syntax

  C.   Pragmatics

  D.   Semantics

Answer: C. Pragmatics
Pragmatics involves the way that language is used to communicate and interact with others. It is often used to control the actions and attitudes of other people.

5. Scott is in middle school but still makes statements like, "I gotted new high-tops yesterday," and "I saw three mans in the front office." Language interventions for Scott would target:
(Average)

  A. Morphology

  B. Syntax

  C. Pragmatics

  D. Semantics

Answer A. Morphology
Students with problems in this area may not use inflectional endings in their words, may not be consistent in their use of certain morphemes, or may be delayed in learning such morphemes as irregular past tenses.

6. Which component of language involves language content rather than the form of language?
(Rigorous)

  A. Phonology

  B. Morphology

  C. Semantics

  D. Syntax

Answer: C. Semantics
Semantics is the study of the relationships between words and grammatical forms in a language, and their underlying meaning: the content, rather than the form of language

7. **Which of the following characteristics is probably most related to physical impairments?**
   (Rigorous)

   A.   Lack of physical stamina

   B.   Progressive weakening of muscles

   C.   Impaired motor abilities

   D.   Side effects from treatment

Answer: C. Impaired motor abilities
The other three conditions may exist in persons with other disabilities. Generally, children with physical disabilities display a variety of conditions. Each condition primarily affects one particular system of the body:

- The cardiopulmonary system affects the blood vessels, heart and lungs.
- The musculoskeletal system affects the muscles, bones and joints.
- The neurological system affects the spinal cord, brain and nerves.

Some conditions develop during pregnancy, at birth, or during infancy, due to factors known and unknown. Others occur later due to disease, injury trauma, or other factors. Besides motor disorders, individuals with physical disabilities may also have multi-disabling conditions like concomitant hearing impairments, visual impairments, perceptual disorders, speech defects, behavior disorders, or mental handicaps. Neurological impairments may also affect sensory abilities, cognitive functions, motor performance, and emotional responsiveness.

8. **Jennifer is eight years old and has been diagnosed with Mental Retardation. She exhibits the following characteristics: poor motor development, minimal speech and communication, is not potty trained, and requires constant supervision. How would she be classified in terms of degree of cognitive impairment?**
(Rigorous)

A. Mild

B. Moderate

C. Severe

D. Profound

Answer: C. Severe
Jennifer would most likely fall into the severe category. All categories are as follows:

Mild (IQ of 50–55 to 70)
- Delays in most areas (communication, motor, academic)
- Often not distinguished from normal children until of school age.
- Can acquire both academic and vocational skills; can become self-supporting

Moderate (IQ of 35–40 to 50–55)
- Only fair motor development; clumsy
- Poor social awareness
- Can be taught to communicate
- Can profit from training in social and vocational skills; needs supervision, but can perform semiskilled labor as an adult

Severe (IQ of 20–25 to 35–40)
- Poor motor development
- Minimal speech and communication
- Minimal ability to profit from training in health and self-help skills: may contribute to self-maintenance under constant supervision as an adult

Profound (IQ below 20–25)
- Gross retardation, both mental and sensor-motor
- Little or no development of basic communication skills
- Dependency on others to maintain basic life functions
- Lifetime of complete supervision (institution, home, nursing home)

9. Otumba is a 16 year old in your class who recently came from Nigeria. The girls in your class have come to you to complain about the way he treats them in a sexist manner. When they complain you reflect that this is also the way he treats adult females. You have talked to Otumba before about appropriate behavior. You should first:
    (Rigorous)

    A.   Complain to the Principal

    B.   Ask for a Parent-Teacher Conference

    C.   Check to see if this is a cultural norm in his country

    D.   Create a behavior contract for him to follow

Answer: C. Check to see if this is a cultural norm in his country
While choices A, B, and D are appropriate actions, it is important to remember that Otumba comes from a culture where woman are treated differently than they are here in America. Learning this information will enable the school as a whole to address this behavior.

10. Some of the factors that can contribute to learning disabilities and/or cognitive impairments include problems with fetal brain development, genetic factors, environmental factors, problems during pregnancy or delivery, environmental toxins, and the use of drugs or alcohol during pregnancy. Which of the following conditions can be directly related to one of the above listed factors?
    (Easy)

    A.   Emotional Disturbance

    B.   Fetal Alcohol Syndrome

    C.   Learning Disability

    D.   Attention Deficit Disorder

Answer: B. Fetal Alcohol Syndrome
Heavy alcohol use during pregnancy has been linked to Fetal Alcohol Syndrome (FAS), a condition resulting in low birth weight, intellectual impairment, hyperactivity, and certain physical defects.

11. Statements like, "Darren is lazy," are not helpful in describing his behavior for all but which of these reasons?
(Rigorous)

   A.   There is no way to determine if any change occurs from the information given

   B.   The student and not the behavior becomes labeled

   C.   Darren's behavior will manifest itself clearly enough without any written description

   D.   Such labels are open to various interpretations among the people who are asked to define them

Answer: C. Darren's behavior will manifest itself clearly enough without any written description
"Darren is lazy" is a label. It can be interpreted in a variety of ways, and there is no way to measure this description for change. A description should be measurable. In addition, this label focuses upon the child, not the behavior to be assessed.

12. Criteria for choosing behaviors that most need change involve all but the following:
(Average)

   A.   Observations across settings to rule out certain interventions

   B.   Pinpointing the behavior that is the poorest fit in the child's environment

   C.   The teacher's concern about what is the most important behavior to target

   D.   Analysis of the environmental reinforcers

Answer: C. The teacher's concern about what is the most important behavior to target
Choices A, B, and D are more objective measures of the behavior and its effects. As such, it is these that should be the focus of the teacher's efforts. The teacher should focus her/his concern on objective measures of behavior.

13. **Measuring frequency is appropriate for all of these behaviors EXCEPT:**
    (Rigorous)

    A.   Teasing

    B.   Talking out

    C.   Being on time for class

    D.   Off-task behavior

Answer: D. Off-task behavior
Off-task behavior is relevant because it reduces time on task or engaged learning time. Therefore, it is better measured by duration.

14. **Which is generally true about students with mild disabilities?**
    (Easy)

    A.   Comprise about half of the total special education population

    B.   Are generally recognized once they begin school and have learning challenges

    C.   Have a high school dropout rate

    D.   All of the above

Answer: D. All of the above
This population is no different physically from other students, so their disabilities may not be noticed until the requirements of school begin. They do drop out of school at a higher rate than the non-disabled students do, and they comprise about half of the population of students with disabilities.

15. Which of the following is true about autism?
(Rigorous)

A.   It is caused by having cold, aloof or hostile parents

B.   Approximately 4 out of 10 people have autism

C.   It is a Separate Exceptionality Category in IDEA

D.   It is a form of Mental Illness

Answer: C. It is a Separate Exceptionality Category in IDEA

Smith and Luckasson (1992) describe autism as a severe language disorder that affects thinking, communication, and behavior. They list the following characteristics:

- **Absent or distorted relationships with people**—inability to relate with people except as objects, inability to express affection, or ability to build and maintain only distant, suspicious or bizarre relationships.
- **Extreme or peculiar problems in communication**—absence of verbal language or language that is not functional, such as echolalia (parroting what one hears), misuse of pronouns (e.g. he for you or I for her), neologisms (made-up meaningless words or sentences), talk that bears little or no resemblance to reality.
- **Self-stimulation**—repetitive stereotyped behavior that seems to have no purpose other than providing sensory stimulation. This may take a wide variety of forms, such as swishing saliva, twirling objects, patting one's cheeks, flapping one's arms, staring, etc.
- **Self-injury**—repeated physical self-abuse, such as biting, scratching, or poking oneself, head banging, etc.
- **Perceptual anomalies**—unusual responses or absence of response to stimuli that seem to indicate sensory impairment or unusual sensitivity.

16. In which of the following exceptionality categories may a student be considered for inclusion if his IQ score falls more than two standard deviations below the mean?
(*Average*)

   A.   Mental Retardation

   B.   Specific Learning Disabilities

   C.   Emotionally/Behaviorally Disordered

   D.   Gifted

Answer: A. Mental Retardation
Only about 1 to 1.5% of the population fit the AAMD's definition of mental retardation. They fall outside the 2 standard deviations limit for Special Learning Disabilities and Emotionally/Behaviorally disordered.

17. According to IDEA, a child whose disability is related to being deaf and blind may not be classified as:
(*Rigorous*)

   A.   Multiple Disabilities

   B.   Other Health Impaired

   C.   Mentally Retarded

   D.   Visually Impaired

Answer: A. Multiple Disabilities
The only stated area where deaf-blindness is not accepted is in Multiple Disabilities. Deaf-blind is a separate category on the IDEA classification list, so inclusion in Multiple Disabilities would be redundant.

18. **Legislation in Public Law 94 – 142 attempts to:**
    (Average)

    A.   Match the child's educational needs with appropriate educational services

    B.   Include parents in the decisions made about their child's education

    C.   Establish a means by which parents can provide input

    D.   All of the above

Answer: D. All of the above
Much of what was stated in separate court rulings and mandated legislation was brought together into what is now considered to be the "backbone" of special education. Public Law 94 – 142 (Education for All Handicapped Children Act) was signed into law by President Ford in 1975. It was the culmination of a great deal of litigation and legislation from the late 1960s to the mid-1970s, which included decisions supporting the need to assure an appropriate education to all persons regardless of race, creed, or disability.

In 1990, this law was reauthorized and renamed the Individuals with Disabilities Education Act, IDEA.

19. **The definition of assistive technology devices was amended in the IDEA reauthorization of 2004 to exclude what?**
   (Average)

   A.   iPods and other hand-held devices

   B.   Computer enhanced technology

   C.   Surgically implanted devices

   D.   Braille and/or special learning aids

Answer: C. Surgically implanted devices
The definition of assistive technology devices was amended to exclude devices that are surgically implanted (i.e. cochlear implants), and it clarified that students with assistive technology devices shall not be prevented from having special education services. Assistive technology devices may need to be monitored by school personnel, but schools are not responsible for the surgical implantation or replacement of such devices.

20. **The Individuals with Disabilities Education Act (IDEA) was signed into law in:**
   (Average)

   A.   1975

   B.   1980

   C.   1990

   D.   1995

Answer: C. 1990
IDEA, Public Law 101 – 476 is a consolidation and reauthorization of all prior Special Education mandates, with amendments. It was signed into law by President Bush on October 30, 1990.

21. **Section 504 differs from the scope of IDEA because its main focus is on:**
    (Rigorous)

    A.   Prohibition of discrimination on the basis of disability

    B.   A basis for additional support services and accommodations in a special education setting

    C.   Procedural rights and safeguards for the individual

    D.   Federal funding for educational services

Answer: A. Prohibition of discrimination on the basis of disability
Section 504 prohibits discrimination on the basis of disability.

22. **Satisfaction of the Least Restrictive Environment (LRE) requirement means:**
    (Rigorous)

    A.   The school is providing the best services it can offer

    B.   The school is providing the best services the district has to offer

    C.   The student is being educated with the fewest special education services necessary

    D.   The student is being educated in the least restrictive setting that meets his or her needs

Answer: D. The student is being educated in the least restrictive setting that meets his or her needs
The legislation mandates LRE. Exactly what constitutes LRE for a given child will depend upon his or her individual needs.

23. **What legislation started FAPE?**
    (Rigorous)

    A.   Section 504

    B.   EHCA

    C.   IDEA

    D.   Education Amendment 1974

Answer: A. Section 504
FAPE stands for Free Appropriate Public Education. Section 504 of the Rehabilitation Act in 1973 is the legislation that enacted FAPE. Since that time, it has been expanded and reauthorized in various forms of IDEA (Individuals with Disabilities Education Act).

24. **Which is untrue about the Americans with disabilities Act (ADA)?**
    (Rigorous)

    A.   It was signed into law the same year as IDEA by President Bush

    B.   It reauthorized the discretionary programs of EHA

    C.   It gives protection to all people on the basis of race, sex, national origin, and religion

    D.   It guarantees equal opportunities to persons with disabilities in employment, public accommodations, transportation, government services, and telecommunications

Answer: B. It reauthorized the discretionary programs of EHA
EHA is the precursor of IDEA, the Individuals with Disabilities Education Act. ADA, however, is Public Law 101 – 336, the Americans with Disabilities Act, which gives civil rights protection to all individuals with disabilities in private sector employment, all public services, public accommodations, transportation, and telecommunications. It was patterned after the Rehabilitation Act of 1973.

25. **One of the most important goals of the special education teacher is to foster and create with the student:**
    (Easy)

    A.   Handwriting skills

    B.   Self-advocacy

    C.   An increased level of reading

    D.   Logical reasoning

Answer: B. Self-advocacy
When a student achieves the ability to recognize his/her deficits and knows how to correctly advocate for his/her needs, the child has learned one of the most important life skills.

26. **The best resource a teacher can have to reach a student is:**
    (Rigorous)

    A.   Contact with the parents/guardians

    B.   A successful behavior modification exam

    C.   A listening ear

    D.   Gathered scaffold approach to teaching

Answer: A. Contact with the parents/guardians
Parents are often the best source of information on their children. They generally know if a behavior management technique will be successful.

27. The earliest establishment of organizations whose membership contained professionals in related fields serving individuals with disabilities came from:
(Rigorous)

    A.   Sociology

    B.   Psychology

    C.   Medicine

    D.   All of the Above

Answer: B. Psychology
The American Psychological Association (APA) is a scientific and professional society working to improve mental health services and to advocate for legislation and programs that will promote mental health; facilitate research, and professional development. It was founded at Clark University in 1892 for the advancement of psychology as a science. The association was incorporated in 1925 in Washington, D.C. Some of the early professionals responsible for serving individuals with disabilities are Thomas Hopkins Galludet, Samuel Gridley, Edward Seguin, Louis Terman, Maria Montessori, John B. Watson, and B. F. Skinner.

28. The service medium facility that helps formerly institutionalized clients to adjust while becoming self-supporting members of the community is the: (Rigorous)

    A.   Half-way Residential Home

    B.   Group Home

    C.   Sheltered Workshop

    D.   Foster Family Home

Answer: A. Half-way Residential Home
Half-way residential houses are available in some communities for formerly institutionalized individuals who need support while receiving vocational training and learning to be more independent. These may offer other forms of support, such as daily living skills and social/interpersonal counseling.

29. **Which is a less than ideal example of collaboration for successful inclusion?**
    (Average)

    A.   Special education teachers are part of the instructional team in a regular classroom

    B.   Special education teachers act as assistants to regular education teachers in the classroom

    C.   Teaming approaches are used for problem solving and program implementation

    D.   Regular teachers, special education teachers, and other specialists or support teachers co-teach

Answer: B. Special education teachers act as assistants to regular education teachers in the classroom
Regular education teachers, special education teachers, and other specialists should work collaboratively to provide the best services to the student. Special education teachers should be more than just "assistants" in the regular classroom.

30. **The movement towards serving as many children with disabilities as possible in the regular classroom with supports and services grew out of:**
    (Average)

    A.   The Full Service Model

    B.   The Regular Education Model

    C.   The Normalization movement

    D.   The Mainstream Model

Answer: C. The Normalization movement
The Normalization Movement advocated movement toward less restrictive environments for people with disabilities. It led to deinstitutionalization and the attempt to let people with disabilities live, go to school, and work in an environment as "normal," or as close as possible to that of their peer group without disabilities.

DELIVERY OF SERVICES TO STUDENTS

31. **Cognitive Learning strategies include:**
    (Rigorous)

    A.   Reinforcing appropriate behavior

    B.   Teaching students problem solving and critical thinking skills

    C.   Heavily structuring the learning environment

    D.   Generalizing learning from one setting to another

Answer: B. Teaching students problem solving and critical thinking skills
The Cognitive Learning approach to special education emphasizes measurable outcomes of a student's learning. It is often associated with Bloom's taxonomy of higher level thinking (knowledge, comprehension, application, analysis, and synthesis) and Haladyna's learning processes of understanding, problem solving, critical thinking, and creativity.

32. **Bob shows behavior problems such as lack of attention, out of seat, and talking out. His teacher has kept data on these behaviors and has found that Bob is showing much better self-control since he has been self-managing himself through a behavior modification program. The most appropriate placement recommendation for Bob at this time is probably:**
    (Easy)

    A.   Any available part-time special education program

    B.   The regular classroom solely

    C.   A behavior disorders resource room for one period a day

    D.   A specific learning disabilities resource room for one period a day

Answer: B. The regular classroom solely
Bob is able to self-manage himself and is very likely to behave like the other children in the regular classroom. The regular classroom is the least restrictive environment.

33. A important component of IDEA deals with "Due Process." Due Process a set of procedures designed to ensure fairness and accountability in decisions related to the education of students with disabilities. Which of the following is NOT considered a Due Process right for parents under IDEA?
(Average)

A.   The right to specify which school personnel will work with their child

B.   The right to a Due Process Hearing if they do not agree with the school's recommendations

C.   The right to an Independent Educational Evaluation (IEE)

D.   The right to written notice prior to a prior to a proposal or refusal to initiate or make a change in the child's identification, evaluation, or educational placement

Answer: A. The right to specify which school personnel will work with their child
Assignment of school personnel remains the responsibility of the individual school and is not a component of Due Process according to IDEA.

34. The effective teacher varies her instructional presentations and response requirements depending upon:
(Easy)

A.   Student needs

B.   The task at hand

C.   The learning situation

D.   All of the above

Answer: D. All of the above
Differentiated instruction and meeting the needs of the group as a whole must address the students' modes of learning to be successful.

35. **The following words describe an IEP objective EXCEPT:**
    (Average)

    A.   Specific

    B.   Observable

    C.   Measurable

    D.   Criterion-referenced

Answer: D. Criterion-referenced
An Individual Education Plan (IEP) should be specific, observable, and measurable. Criterion referenced is a term used to define a type of test or assessment.

36. **Which one of the following is NOT a primary purpose of an IEP?**
    (Rigorous)

    A.   To outline instructional programs

    B.   To develop self-advocacy skills

    C.   To function as the basis for evaluation

    D.   To facilitate communication among staff members, teachers, parents, and students

B. To develop self-advocacy skills
While self-advocacy should be encouraged, it is not one of the primary purposes of an IEP. It might, of course, be one of the goals listed for a child, if the IEP team feels it is important to their educational success.

37. _____ is a method used to increase student engaged learning time by having students teach other students.
(Easy)

A. Peer tutoring

B. Engaged learning time

C. Allocated learning time

D. Teacher consultation

Answer: A. Peer tutoring
Peer tutoring is a method for increasing student learning time by having students teach other students. Special care must be taken to be sure students are trained to use this method effectively and without one student feeling superior to another.

38. The Integrated approach to learning utilizes all resources available to address student needs. What are the resources?
(Rigorous)

A. The student, his/her parents, and the teacher.

B. The teacher, the parents, and the special education team.

C. The teacher, the student, and an administrator to perform needed interventions.

D. The student, his/her parents, the teacher, and community resources.

Answer: D. The student, his/her parents, the teacher, and community resources.
The integrated response encompasses all possible resources including the resources in the community.

39. **Cooperative learning uses all these methods, EXCEPT:**
(Average)

    A.   Shared ideas

    B.   Small groups

    C.   Independent practice

    D.   Student expertise

Answer: C. Independent practice
Cooperative learning focuses on group cooperation allowing for sharing of student expertise and provides some flexibility for creative presentation of the students as they share with others.

40. **Presentation of tasks can be altered to match the student's rate of learning by:**
(Rigorous)

    A.   Describing how much of a topic is presented in one day, and how much practice is assigned, according to the student's abilities and learning style

    B.   Using task analysis, assign a certain number of skills to be mastered in a specific amount of time

    C.   Introducing a new task only when the student has demonstrated mastery of the previous task in the learning hierarchy

    D.   A and C

Answer: D. A and C
Pacing is the term used for altering of tasks to match the student's rate of learning. This can be done in two ways: altering the subject content and the rate at which tasks are presented.

41. Alternative response patterns are educationally important because:
(Easy)

A. They allow the special needs student the opportunity to approach a task from a position that best suits his learning style

B. They permit the teacher to use her knowledge of the students' learning styles and capabilities to design the best learning environment for each student

C. They allow all students, even non-readers, to interact in the instructional setting

D. All of the above

Answer: D. All of the above
Instructional alternatives to help students with learning problems may be referred to as compensatory techniques, instructional adaptations, or accommodation techniques. Certain students have difficulty with writing answers but may be able to express their knowledge of subject matter verbally. Therefore, modifications of content area material may be extended to methods and modifications for evaluation and assessment of student progress. Teachers are learning the value of giving assignments that meet the individual abilities and needs of students. After instruction, discussion, questioning, and practice have been provided, rather than assigning one task to all students, teachers are asking students to generate tasks that will show their knowledge of the information presented. Students are given choices and thereby have the opportunity to demonstrate more effectively the skills, concepts, or topics that they as individuals have learned. It has been established that student choice increases student originality, intrinsic motivation, and higher mental processes.

42. **Which type of instructional arrangement established and enhances mutual respect for other students and promotes positive social goals:** *(Rigorous)*

    A.   Homogeneous grouping

    B.   One-on-one instruction

    C.   Cooperative learning

    D.   Small group instruction

Answer: C. Cooperative learning
Cooperative learning techniques can be used to establish and enhance mutual respect for other students. Cooperative learning can promote positive social goals when used effectively as a teaching and learning tool. When the teacher promotes interaction of students among ethnic and social groups, students tend to respond positively by forming friendships and having enhanced respect for other sociological groups. Thus, the teacher who effectively manages cooperative learning groups has not only promoted cognitive learning but has also promoted desirable behaviors in terms of mutual respect for all students.

43. **Functional skills include _____ skills.** *(Easy)*

    A.   personal-social

    B.   daily living

    C.   occupational readiness

    D.   All of the above

Answer: D. All of the above
A transition or vocational curriculum approach focuses upon what students need to learn that will be useful to them and prepare them for functioning in society as adults. Life preparation includes not only occupational readiness but also personal-social and daily living skills.

44. In career education, specific training and preparation required for the world of work occurs during the phase of:
(Easy)

A.   Career Awareness

B.   Career Exploration

C.   Career Preparation

D.   Daily Living and Personal-Social Interaction

Answer: C. Career Preparation
Curricular aspects of career education include:

- Career Awareness: diversity of available jobs
- Career Exploration: skills needed for occupational groups
- Career Preparation: specific training and preparation required for the world of work

45. For which stage of learning would computer software be utilized that allows for continued drill and practice of a skill to achieve accuracy and speed?
(Average)

A.   Acquisition

B.   Proficiency

C.   Maintenance

D.   Generalization

Answer: B. Proficiency
The definition for the above terms are:

- **Acquisition**—Introduction of a new skill.
- **Maintenance**—Continued practice without further instruction.
- **Proficiency**—Practice under supervision to achieve accuracy and speed.
- **Generalization**—Application of the new skills in new settings and situations.

46. **When a student begins to use assistive technology, it is important for the teacher to have a clear outline as to when and how the equipment should be used. Why?**
(Rigorous)

   A.   To establish a level of accountability with the student

   B.   To establish that the teacher has responsibility for the equipment that is in use in his/her room

   C.   To establish that the teacher is responsible for the usage of the assistive technology

   D.   To establish a guideline for evaluation

Answer: A. To establish a level of accountability with the student
Clear parameters as to the usage of assistive technology in a classroom create a level of accountability in the student. Both the student and the teacher should know the intended purpose and appropriate manner of use of the device.

47. **Which is characteristic of standardized group tests?**
(Rigorous)

   A.   Directions are always read to students

   B.   The examiner monitors several students at the same time

   C.   The teacher is allowed to probe students who almost have the correct answer

   D.   Both quantitative and qualitative information may be gathered

Asnwer: B. The examiner monitors several students at the same time
In standardized group tests, directions and procedures are carefully prescribed and scripted. Children write or mark their own responses. The examiner monitors the progress of several children at the same time. He cannot rephrase questions or probe or prompt responses. It is very difficult to obtain qualitative information from standardized group tests. Standardized group tests are appropriate for program evaluation, screening, and some types of program planning, such as tracking. Special consideration may need to be given if there are any motivational, personality, linguistic, or physically disabling factors that might impair the examinee's performance. When planning individual programs, individual tests should be used.

48. **Which of the following types of tests is used to estimate learning potential and to predict academic achievement?**
(Easy)

   A.   Intelligence Tests

   B.   Achievement Tests

   C.   Adaptive Behavior Tests

   D.   Personality Tests

Answer: A. Intelligence Tests
An intelligence test is designed to measure intellectual abilities like memory, comprehension, and abstract reasoning. IQ is often used to estimate the learning capacity of a student as well as to predict academic achievement.

49. **In exceptional student education, assessment is used to make decisions about all of the following except:**
(Average)

   A.   Screening and initial identification of children who may need services

   B.   Selection and evaluation of teaching strategies and programs

   C.   Determining the desired attendance rate of a student

   D.   Development of goals, objectives, and evaluation for the IEP

Answer: C. Determining the desired attendance rate of a student
School attendance is required, and assessment is not necessary to measure a child's attendance rate.

50. **Children who write poorly might be given tests that allow oral responses, unless the purpose for giving the test is to:**
(Easy)

   A.   Assess handwriting skills

   B.   Test for organization of thoughts

   C.   Answer questions pertaining to math reasoning

   D.   Assess rote memory

A. Assess handwriting skills
It is necessary to have the child write if we are assessing their skill in that domain.

51. **Alternative assessments include all of the following EXCEPT:**
(Average)

   A.   Portfolios

   B.   Interviews

   C.   Textbook chapter tests

   D.   Student choice of assessment format

C. Textbook chapter tests
Textbook chapter tests are formal, usually multiple choice tests with one fixed, correct answer. Choices A, B, and D are alternative methods of assessment.

52. **According to Mercer and Mercer, what would be an appropriate amount of homework for a student in fourth grade:**
   (Average)

   A.   15 minutes, 3 days a week

   B.   45–75 minutes, 5 days a week

   C.   75–120 minutes, 5 days a week

   D.   15–45 minutes, 2 to 4 days a week

Answer: D. 15–45 minutes, 2 to 4 days a week
The following are recommended times for students in regular education classes:

- **Primary Grades**—three 15-minutes assignments per week
- **Grades 4 to 6**—two to four 15 to 45-minute assignments per week
- **Grades 7 to 9**—as many as five 45 to 75-minute assignments per week
- **Grades 10 to 12**—as many as five 75 to 120 minute assignments per week

Homework assignments may need to be modified for some students with disabilities. Some students with disabilities may be unable to handle the usual amount of homework. Care should be taken to ensure that the homework practice is *practice*, not new learning. Like many aspects of instruction, homework should be differentiated.

53. **Mr. Brown finds that his chosen consequence does not seem to be having the desired effect of reducing the target misbehavior. Which of these would LEAST LIKELY account for Mr. Brown's lack of success with the consequence?**
(Easy)

  A. The consequence was aversive in Mr. Brown's opinion but not the students'

  B. The students were not developmentally ready to understand the connection

  C. Mr. Brown was inconsistent in applying the consequence

  D. The intervention had not previously been shown to be effective in studies

Answer: D. The intervention had not previously been shown to be effective in studies
Choices A, B, and C might work if applied in the classroom, but research is less relevant in this situation than the specific elements of Mr. Brown's class.

54. **When would proximity control not be a good behavioral intervention?**
(Easy)

  A. Two students are arguing

  B. A student is distracting others

  C. One student threatens another

  D. Involve fading and shaping

Answer: C. One student threatens another
Threats can break into fights. Standing in the middle of a fight can be threatening to your ability to supervise the class as a whole or to get the help needed to stop the fight.

55. **Katie frequently is disruptive prior to each day's math lesson. From a behavior management perspective, the math lesson appears to be the _____ to Katie's undesirable disruptive behavior.**
(Average)

   A.   subsequent development

   B.   succeeding force

   C.   consequence

   D.   antecedent

Answer: D. antecedent
Antecedents are the causes of behaviors, and they therefore precede the behavior. The special educator should be aware of antecedents to undesirable behaviors. These may include a time of day, a particular activity, a location, or a combination of people. While some upsetting situations may be avoided, it is often important to work with the student so that the situation is more tolerable.

56. **The best way to ensure the success of educational interventions is to:**
(Average)

   A.   Give regular education teachers the primary responsibility of teaching special needs students in regular classrooms

   B.   Give special education teachers the primary responsibility of teaching special needs students in special education classrooms

   C.   Promote cooperative teaching efforts between general and special educators

   D.   Have support personnel assume the primary responsibility for the education of special needs students

Answer: C. Promote cooperative teaching efforts between general and special educators
Both types of teachers can learn from each other, and students can learn from each other and become sensitive to the special needs of each other.

57. **In regard to the influence of teacher attitudes, which of the following is critical in the successful inclusion of the student with a disability:** *(Average)*

   A.   The special education teacher should take full responsibility for the student with a disability

   B.   The student with a disability only attend special events with the general education classroom

   C.   Special education and regular education teachers should demonstrate the attitude that the exceptional student is a student of both teachers, not a special education student who only goes into a general education classroom at certain times

   D.   The general education should wait for the special education teacher to be in the classroom before interacting with the student

Answer: C. Special education and regular education teachers should demonstrate the attitude that the exceptional student is a student of both teachers, not a special education student who only goes into a general education classroom at certain times

One of the key factors in successful inclusion is the attitude that the student is a true member of the classroom and a student of both teachers.

Which of the following would promote a good working relationship with a paraprofessional who has been assigned to your classroom? *(Average)*

A. Having the paraprofessional grade papers

B. Telling the paraprofessional what you expect him/her to do

C. Offering support to paraprofessionals by observing their work with students and offering feedback and suggestions

D. Asking the paraprofessional to sit in the back of the room and only interact with students when you direct them.

Answer: C. Offering support to paraprofessionals by observing their work with students and offering feedback and suggestions
CEC suggests that teachers can best collaborate with general education teachers and paraprofessionals by:

- Offering information about the characteristics and needs of children with exceptional learning needs
- Discussing and brainstorming ways to integrate children with exceptionalities into various settings within the school community
- Modeling best practices and instructional techniques and accommodations and coaching others in their use
- Keeping communication about children with exceptional learning needs and their families confidential
- Consulting with these colleagues in the assessment of individuals with exceptional learning needs
- Engaging them in group problem-solving and in developing, executing, and assessing collaborative activities
- Offering support to paraprofessionals by observing their work with students and offering feedback and suggestions

59. **Related service providers include all of the following EXCEPT:**
(Average)

    A.   General education teachers

    B.   Speech and language therapists

    C.   Occupational therapists

    D.   Psychologists

Answer: A. General education teachers
General education teachers are important collaborators with teachers of exceptional students; however, they are not related service providers. Related service providers offer specialized skills and abilities that are critical to an exceptional education teacher's ability to advocate for his or her student and meet a school's legal obligations to the student and his or her family. Related service providers, such as speech, occupational, and language therapists and psychologists, offer expertise and resources unparalleled in meeting a child's developmental needs.

60. **In conducting a parent conference, the teacher should address each of the following EXCEPT:**
(Easy)

    A.   Provide samples of student work and other relevant information

    B.   Focus on observable behaviors

    C.   Offer suggestions for better parenting

    D.   Be a good listener

Answer: C. Offer suggestions for better parenting
As you address issues or areas of concern, be sure to focus on observable behaviors and concrete results or information. Do not make judgmental statements about parent or child. Share specific work samples, anecdotal records of behavior, etc., that demonstrate clearly the concerns you have. Be a good listener and hear the parent's comments and explanations.

ANSWER KEY

1.	A		31.	B
2.	B		32.	B
3.	D		33.	A
4.	C		34.	D
5.	A		35.	D
6.	C		36.	B
7.	C		37.	A
8.	C		38.	D
9.	C		39.	C
10.	B		40.	D
11.	C		41.	D
12.	C		42.	C
13.	D		43.	D
14.	D		44.	C
15.	C		45.	B
16.	A		46.	A
17.	A		47.	B
18.	D		48.	A
19.	C		49.	C
20.	C		50.	A
21.	A		51.	C
22.	D		52.	D
23.	A		53.	D
24.	B		54.	C
25.	B		55.	D
26.	A		56.	C
27.	B		57.	C
28.	A		58.	C
29.	B		59.	A
30.	C		60.	C

RIGOR TABLE

	Easy 23%	Average 37%	Rigorous 40%
Question	10, 14, 25, 32, 34, 37, 41, 43, 44, 48, 50, 53, 54, 60	1, 3, 5, 12, 16, 18, 19, 20, 29, 30, 33, 35, 39, 45, 49, 51, 52, 55, 56, 57, 58, 59	2, 4, 6, 7, 8, 9, 11, 13, 15, 17, 21, 22, 23, 24, 26, 27, 28, 31, 36, 38, 40, 42, 46, 47,

CPSIA information can be obtained at www.ICGtesting.com
Printed in the USA
BVOW06s0758021214

377567BV00007B/202/P